One

One Minute, Please?

Cole Schafer

HOLON
Publishing

Pretty souls that have inspired me.

Trey Schafer. Holly Goldzwig. Ian Holbrook. Susan Hyatt.
John Wahoski. Alex Malhotra. Luke Powell. Auston Pugh.
Robert Lucas. Jeremy Raley. Mariya Leona. Kaleb Jordan.
Hannah Woosley Angel. Bethany Bauman. Jack Danks.
Rita Sater. Conner Schafer. Chris Schafer. Brian Grant.
Taylor Mathis. Laila Rayes-Schafer. Robbie Graninger.
Taylor Silke. Eminence Tennyson. Colleen Watters.
Michael Payne. Mackenzie Alcorn. Akanksha Rana.
Alexandra Bacchus. Blake Swanger. Johnna Slaby.
Jaclyn Neville. Sara Riester. Mary Wullschleger.
Amber Pretzsch. Taylor Duran. Clair Strobel.
Genesis Robinson. Maya Sater. Lucas Bartnick.
Adrianna O'Daniel. Morgan Thewes. Zack Mathis.
Megan Montgomery. Megan Evans. Jordyn Moore.
Kayla Butrum. Jake Jones. Jacob Tilmon. John Pena.
Heather Campbell. Sarah Hasenour. Brandon Scott.
Olivia Bullock. Hamilton Reagan. Cheyenne Ramsey.
Amelia Weiss. Lexi Taylor. Chris Schultheis. Jake Titzer.
Kirsten Grenier. Tristan Chancellor. Evan Davis. Mia Cooper.
Kacey Jane. Mary Grace Ramsey. Taylor Mcferran. Bradie Gray.
Whitney Odum. Sarah Memmer. Nathan Fox. Lauren Reveley.
Candace Young. Emily Branstrom. Madie Ratliff. Abhi Mishra.
Alex Santiago. Molly Gilles. Megan Gresham. Holland Colvin.
Sheridan Strickland. Candace Belle Brickey. George Suggs.
Nikisha Ware. Hannah Kirkpatrick.

Leigh Anne Theuerkauf. Jasmine Bivens. Eddie Shleyner
Max Clemons. Grace Leon. Ellie Lucy. Kumiko Wilkison.
Keaton Weil. Lauren Lee. Ernie Duncan. Katerina Miras.
Leslie Rogers. Erin Graninger. Kyle Hoeing. Chris Wilkison.
Cody Parks. Karah Johnson. Megan Kershaw. Jordan Woods.
Ellen Bennett. Zane Wilkison. Nadia Gravely. Alex Kixmiller.
Marley Stratman. Sean Stone. Blake Malicoat. Austen Henson.
Tanner Maurer. Mitchell Sasseman. Nate Billa. Aubrey Marcus.
Mike Spadier. Andrew Bankson. Alexus Kelley. Alisha White.
Aly Thielges. Naomi Seifert. Natalie Vera. Dania Maaliki.
Victoria Richmond. Jackie Ellsperman. Brooke Valentine.
Virginia Woolf. Ernest Hemingway. Rupi Kaur. Gabrielle
Emma Groffsky. Nico De Bryun. Nicole Whetstine.
Peyton Ahrens. Emily Schuster. Jeremy Gotwals.
Justin Vernon. Frank Ocean. Frank Sinatra.
Billie Eilish. Amy Winehouse. Austin Post.
Greg Gonzalez. Neil Gaiman. Stephen King.
Bonheur "Coco" Chanel. Anne Lamott.
Steven Pressfield. David Ogilvy. Tony Pauley.
Timothy Ferriss. Noah Kagan. Elizabeth Grant.
Debbie Millman. Seth Godin. Brian Koppelman.
Katie Romano. Julia Boyd. Austin Wolf. Shawn Romano.
Kayman Coloso. Pam Rickenbaugh. Ken Town. Steven Rayes.
Ashley Swanger. Nora Sermez. Hazel Behrens. Ashley Conkling.
Hannah Greene. Justin Riat. Mitsuko Ijima.

One Minute, Please?

To be candid,
I'm not entirely sure
what the fuck
any of this is about.

But,

if you have a minute...

I do think I can make
you feel something.

–Cole.

Give yourself a physical.

I think it's wise to give yourself a physical from time to time. Not the fondle your testicles nor knead your breasts kind. Though, I think that'd be wise, too. I'm referring to a life physical.

The one where you lock yourself in your room on a quiet Sunday and leave the distractions on the other side of the door. The one where you let your mind wander and worry. The one where you force yourself to ask perhaps the most important question you'll ever ask...

Am I living the life I want to be living?

I'd assume most people go twenty, thirty and even forty years never asking themselves that question, never spending an hour locked in a room, forced into their own thoughts in a world where their opinion is the only opinion that matters.

The cost? They live lives where their opinion is the only opinion that doesn't matter and that's cancerous.

—Cole.

Cleo.

Let's

    get

        naked

            and

                build

                   an

                        empire.

–Cole.

John Wayne.

Before my grandmother dropped dead
from a massive aneurysm
she used to tell me about John Wayne.
It was an ironic obsession of hers,
considering she was one-hundred-percent Japanese,
and the Hollywood cowboy was white as white could be.
But, I think she saw herself in the
lead-slinging venom-blooded mustang-wrangler
that'd ride like a banshee through the wild wild west.
The ship she rode to America was her horse
and she was John Wayne.
Five years have passed since she's been gone
and her conversations play from time to time
near the back of my skull like old vinyl.
When I find myself intimidated by one of life's horses,
she'll pipe in with her Japanese accent.
She'll remind me not to be scared.
She'll remind me I'm John Wayne.

She'd want me to remind you that you're John Wayne, too.

–Cole.

Chandelier.

Women like her
were born to be
the centerpiece

of
       every
           room
               they
                    step
                        foot
                             in.

—Cole.

The fine line between love and obsession.

I'm an advocate of self-love, an enemy of self-obsession. Most of what
we see today in this virtual world we play in is not self-love but self-
obsession. Men and women throw a mask on it and call it self-love, but
it's not. When you love yourself, that light shines through, it beams out
of you penetrating into the hearts and minds of others, inspiring them
to love themselves too. When you're obsessed with yourself, you produce
no light, only darkness. Self-obsessed people want the world darker so
they can burn brighter. To put it in less abstract terms, when someone
stumbles into you (be it in the physical or virtual world) will they leave
feeling fuller, stronger, lovelier? Or, will they leave feeling less? That is the
fundamental difference between self-love and self-obsession. Those who
love themselves show others how to love themselves too.

–Cole.

Unbuttoned.

She
smiled
and
bit
her
bottom
lip
and
my
denim
went
taut.

—Cole.

The French Exit.

The French Exit, also commonly referred to as an Irish Goodbye, is the act of leaving a social gathering without a formal farewell.

It's escaping the party through the backdoor without so much as a peep. I've come to be quite fond of the French Exit. For various reasons, but mostly because I find great pain in acknowledging something good has come to a close.

Leaving her life has been the hardest thing I've ever done. And, I know she doesn't think so because I exited through the back door with little more than a wave goodbye. But, if I would have stopped the music, I'm not entirely sure the party would have continued on. And, I'd like to think it's still going strong without me. I'd like to think she's still going strong without me. I'd like to think she's still going strong without me because she's incredibly fucking strong and will always have great taste in music.

But, excuse my French. I believe it's time for me to make my exit.

—Cole.

Pillows talk.

Listen to your sleepless nights,

our pillows
have a way
of unveiling
our fears
and desires
and dreams.

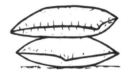

–Cole.

Surprise Birthday Party.

I do find myself wondering from time to time if people lack happiness
because they feel they don't deserve it.

It's not unlike the surprise birthday party thrown for the gent that hates
surprise birthday parties.

He'll laugh and carry on but behind his drunk smiling face he's wrestling
with a nasty question…

Why do all these people care so much about me?

Folks lacking happiness are the same folks who hate surprises, deep down
they feel they're a luxury they don't deserve.

—Cole.

The spins.

Hold me tight,
do anything,
to make
the world
stop spinning.

—Cole.

It's not a trick of the light.

When we're aroused our pupils dilate. They expand. It's a natural unconscious reaction that allows our eyes to absorb as much information as possible about the angel face in front of us. When you notice your best friend's eyes light up when she walks into the room, it's no coincidence. It's not a trick of the light. You're watching his eyes transform to better see his human. I'm a romantic but I think these are some of the most beautiful moments we have. Watching our people fall for their people. Watching something in their eyes change.

–Cole.

A bit lost.

I liked the way she looked when she thought no one was looking...

a bit lost but confident despite her lostness.

–Cole.

Holbrook.

One of my
favorite humans
in the world
is a gent
by the name of
Ian Holbrook.

The most valuable
lesson
he has ever taught
me
is to leave people
better than you find
them.

I'm not certain of
many things.

But, what I do know
is that if more
people
adopted this
philosophy,

*the world would be a
prettier place.*

−Cole.

ijima.

I've grown to love

the cracks

in my porcelain.

–Cole.

It's primal.

The drive to create is ingrained in
our DNA. It's primal.

We want to rip each other's clothes
off because deep down we know
it's why we're all here… we were
created to keep creating.

Yet, I don't believe this drive to
create life exists solely in the form of sex.
I believe we're driven to create life in the form of work, too.

Some of us are driven to build businesses,
design clothes, write books or cook food.

Others are driven to love people, make
them look beautiful or help them feel more confident.

Regardless, in all of us is a piece of work we're driven to create…
a change in the world we see behind closed eyes…
new life we dream of breathing breath into.

We ignore it, pretending it's not there,
but it's just as much a part of us as our hearts and our lungs are.

Sooner or later, we must give in,
we must accept that to create is to be human.

And, that to ignore it is the only sin.

−Cole.

Prettier.

I've been a lot of places,
seen a lot of faces.

Trust me,
my love,
when I say:

this world is far prettier with you in it.

—Cole.

Palatable.

Stop comparing your physical appearance to others. Our tastes in people aren't unlike our tastes in food. They're diverse. Take pizza, burgers, fries, sushi, tacos, pasta and ice cream for example. They're all delicious yet wildly different and it's difficult (maybe even impossible) to say any one is better than the other. Unless you're dealing with a picky person, most everyone is going to find you stunning or at the very least palatable in your own unique way. So, collectively, I think we should stop having dinner with picky people. And, yes, perhaps, it's far-fetched to make comparisons between humans and food but if you were to ask a lion it'd feel differently.

–Cole.

Cascade.

In the mornings
she would climb on top of him
and let loose her hair
and it would fall
like cascading water
around his neck and his face
and his ears and the top of his head,
like a silent waterfall
it would muffle out the sun
soaking through the blinds
and the noise of the city
and the fears that come with living
and in that cocoon
they'd exist,
just the two of them,
sitting so still
as the rest of the world
spun on.

–Cole.

Nothing good gets away.

These things take time,
said the old man.

I don't have time,
said the young boy.

No, you don't have patience,
said the old man,
you have all the time in the world.

The boy sat silent for a moment next to the old man,
drawing something in the dirt with a broken stick,
I suppose I'm worried if I don't move fast enough, she'll get away.

The old man took a long pull from his tobacco pipe,
exhaled,
leaned back,
letting the morning sun warm his cheekbones,
in the words of the late great Steinbeck my dear boy,

'nothing good gets away'.

–Cole.

Blurred lines.

Afternoon sunlight
dancing through
the blinds casting
shadows on your
naked skin; my
favorite motion
picture.

–Cole.

Works-in-progress.

When we remember that the people we stumble
into on a day to day basis are all
just works-in-progress, it gives us permission to have
greater patience, compassion and love towards
them. Not unlike ourselves, they're trying to pilot
the plane while they build it. They're learning as
they go. Failing more often than succeeding.
And, at times, finding themselves desperately
close to giving up. If we have one single
responsibility as humans, it's to love (or at the
very least respect) one another through this
work-in-progress. It's being empathetic
to the fact that nobody is exactly who they want to be,
nor where they want to be, but they're working
like hell to get there.

—Cole.

Sapiosexual.

She

     and

         I

          sipped

              coffee,

                quietly

               watching

          as

         our

     minds

made

love.

—Cole.

The affair.

Inspiration is a bad companion but a brilliant lover. She'll show up for no rhyme or reason. Often times late at night while you're lying wide-eyed in bed. Your thoughts circling like a grand carousel. She'll knock on your front door, careful not to chip her pretty black fingernails. You'll open it to her angel face waiting with a bottle of cheap red wine. And, something lovely to smoke. Until twilight you and she will dance. And, if you're in sync you'll create something that might not change the world. But perhaps a few people in it. Come morning, she'll be gone. Only to return again on another restless night to wrestle you naked, whilst the two of you build an empire. Inspiration for the creative is a bad companion but a brilliant lover. You should love her. You should fuck her. You should miss her when she's gone. But, you shouldn't ever rely on her. Nor build a career around her. Not if you're wanting to make a living in this game. And, you should especially not fall in love with her.

Knock. Knock.

—Cole.

Present.

Devour the moment.
Devour the moment.
Devour the moment.
Devour the moment.
Devour the moment.
Devour the moment.

–Cole.

Eugene.

I had two gin & tonics and called an Uber. Eugene, an African American gent in his mid 60s picked me up and I sat quietly in the car looking out the window at the Nashville Skyline. Eugene had a calmness about him that was difficult to describe. Being in his presence made you feel like the world was spinning slower in a sort of sunny Saturday afternoon kind of way. His voice sounded like something you'd hear on a meditation cassette. I asked Eugene what he did for a living, besides drive Uber, and not to my surprise he said he was a therapist. I asked him if that was why his voice sounded the way it did and he said yes. He said when you talk to people whose worlds are burning down you keep your voice quiet, steady, still and consistent. He said your voice controls the energy in the room and in many ways it controls the emotions of the individual in front of you. Moments later we pulled up to my stop. I got out of the car, and before I shut the door I told him I thought he was a great therapist. He nodded, smiled, and drove off. Still to this day, I'm not sure if Eugene drives Uber because he has to or because he's out late at night putting out fires. I'd guess the latter.

–Cole.

(Lie) Next to me.

I know you're tired.

I am too.

So, let's just lie here.

Let's pretend we're not guilty of the other's exhaustion.

–Cole.

Creative Jesus.

She was creative.
But, not like the others.
She was creative because she had to be creative.
She was creative out of necessity; out of survival.
She eyed the room and the people in it as if it were all familiar.
Like she had spent all her life making art out of broken things.
There was a sadness there.
But, there was also hope.
She grew up with broken things and was once a broken thing.
But, when the other kids went to church, she found Jesus in her creativity.
That was her savior.
I learned something, standing there watching her watch the world.
With that gaze that seemed to hold it all together.
I learned that in some rare instances, creativity saves lives.
And, that if there is a supreme deity, she'd tell us to make good art.

−Cole.

Butterfly stings.

All that's standing in the way of you and me are butterflies.

But, believe me when I say their wings are big and flap hard.

They can hiss and I'm fairly certain the fuckers bite, too.

Did you see that last one?

It just spit fire.

And… and…

My god, you just look so pretty standing over there.

–Cole.

Despicable fabrication.

When you hate someone,

be certain you're hating them,

not the fabricated version of them

you've created in your head.

–Cole.

King of the castle.

I used to decorate my demons
and let them collect dust
in the corners of my room,
but I eventually found out
they don't get any prettier
nor any less obtrusive.

So, I put up the lipstick
and grabbed for the duster
and faced them.

The bunch of us went to war
for a good while,
they fed me plenty of scars
and at one point
I thought I wasn't going to make it.

But, I did.
I'm still here.
And, they're still in my room
but now their heads are mounted
and I'm the king of the castle.

—Cole.

Shhh.

Don't
take
my
silence
for
weakness,

my
quiet
will
move
mountains.

–Cole.

How lovely we have it.

I'm thankful for banana flavored ice cream, damn good sushi and copper cold Kentucky Mules. I'm thankful for pretty girls and pretty friends and watching pretty friends fall in love with pretty girls (I'm looking at you John, Brian and Robbie). I'm thankful for warm conversation at underground arcade bars. I'm thankful for the black heart emoji and hope one day Apple decides to make a porcelain one. I'm thankful for Frank Ocean, Bon Iver, Johnny Cash, Childish Gambino, The National, Amy Winehouse, Barenaked Ladies (and bare naked ladies), Borns, The Weeknd, The Tallest Man on Earth, Bob Marley, Bob Dylan and some fucking talented muscian that will one day light up the whole goddamn world, Trey Schafer. I'm thankful for being born in Southern Indiana and raised by a mother who is as fierce (and lovely) as a valkyrie. I'm thankful for books and words and iced coffee. I'm thankful for fucking my foot to pieces late in my highschool basketball career because if I hadn't I don't think I'd ever become a writer. I'm thankful for fireside whisky-infused ukulele riffs with Ian Holbrook. I'm thankful for Nathan Fox and I's shared love of anime. I'm thankful for my grandmother and the pain that comes with missing her and I'm thankful to have known someone so special that it hurts like hell when they make their French Exit. I'm thankful for the times my brother and I get higher than a pair of kites and we whip up something fucking brilliant on the grill. I'm thankful for you reading this right now because if you got this far, it means you cared enough to give me a minute of your time. And, if you got this far, you should also know that there is a lot to be thankful for even if right now you don't see it. And, sometimes, it helps me to make a list, like the one you're reading now. And, other times, it helps me to take a deep breath and hold it in, and let it out and do it again and again and again and think to myself… *God or the universe or evolution, thank you for giving me these lungs to breathe with and thank you for giving me lovely moments and people and memories that take my fucking breath away.*

—*Cole.*

Spring hollies.

I

    have

       a

         pending

           coffee

             date

               with

                 a

                   snow

                      angel

                        and

                          a

                            p
                            a
                            r
                            t

           of me is terrified

        it's

            all

               going

                  to

                  melt
                  away.

–Cole.

33.

What were you saying about divine intervention?

I was having coffee with a friend and brought up divine intervention. She rolled her eyes and called bullshit. She said if there was a God, he or she or it had better things to do than flirt with miracles in the human realm. I told her I thought it was weird she was calling it a human realm, and to stop talking like we were in fucking Lord of the Rings. And, to that remark, she laughed mid-sip of coffee and spewed it out to the right of the table to avoid drenching me (which I very much appreciated). Instead, she drenched a good looking stranger walking past in shorts. He turned around horrified to find his bare legs covered in coffee, milk, sugar and her saliva. The terrified looks on both their faces transformed into something more like awe as they took in one another's faces. The two of them locked eyes for a long while (or for what seemed like a long while) and I could tell their worlds or human realms had stopped in the way that worlds and realms do when we first lock eyes with our people. I grabbed my coat, stood up, handed him a napkin and motioned to my empty seat. As I left, I looked at my friend, smiled and asked…

Now, what were you saying about divine intervention?

—Cole.

What you could do today to find happiness tomorrow...

You
could
start
worrying
less
about
tomorrow
and
more
about
today.

—Cole.

Scar lit.

Earlier this year an old friend of mind put a gun
to his head and pulled the trigger. While the blast
scattered the demons howling in his skull, I
imagine they found new homes in the hearts of
the loved ones he left behind.

When I heard the news, all I could think about
was kickball, four square and tetherball, the
games we used to play together during recess.

As the years passed we'd chat from time to time,
but not nearly enough. And, eventually, things
ended as most childhood friendships do, we lost
touch with one another.

I remember him smiling a lot growing up.
Shame on me for assuming he would grow up to
be a smiling adult, too. If I could, I would go back
in time before he pulled the trigger and I would
ask him out to lunch. I would tell him when the
demons cry he could come talk to me.

I would tell him that he meant something to me
and the rest of the world and that I think he
should stick around a little while longer.

I would tell him that the world was prettier with
him in it.

–Cole.

Please read this.

You are more powerful than you think you are.
You **are** more powerful than you think you are.
You are **more** powerful than you think you are.
You are more **powerful** than you think you are.
You are more powerful **than** you think you are.
You are more powerful than **you** think you are.
You are more powerful than you **think** you are.
You are more powerful than you think **you** are.
You are more powerful than you think you **are.**

—Cole.

Lovely.

She was pretty fucking

lovely.

Like, I hope she doesn't catch me searching the ceiling for mistletoes,

lovely.

Like, I wish she'd slip in those Doc Martens and fall into my arms,

lovely.

—Cole.

How to talk to people.

1. Listen.
2. Look them in the eyes (I struggle here).
3. Set your phone on silent & leave it face down on the table.
4. Don't make small talk (everyone knows it's cold).
5. Listen.
6. Don't agree just for the sake of agreeing.
7. Don't disagree just for the sake of disagreeing.
8. Listen.
9. Say something interesting.
10. Leave them better than you found them.
11. Listen.

−Cole.

Something iced.

if you've ever
splashed cream into
iced coffee, you've
seen magic unfold as
an explosion of
textures and tones
burst and dance as the
two liquids find
balance in the glass

her eyes were that color.

   *–Cole.*

Until the plane shakes.

Work seems so important…
Money seems so important…
Status seems so important…
Legacy seems so important…

Until the plane shakes.

–Cole.

Why decisions hurt like hell.

Decisions hurt—
they hurt because they're only necessary
when we want two of something
but can only have one.

The word decision
stems from the latin word decidere—
which literally means to cut off.

When you're deciding,
you're not just gaining something,
you're also taking something away.

You're removing it.
You're eliminating it.
You're cutting it off.

Decisions hurt like hell because,
perhaps,
we lose a part of ourselves when we make them.

And, perhaps that's why none of us are whole.

–Cole.

More or less.

I couldn't tell you what I fear
more. Spending the rest of my life
with just one person. Or, never
finding one person I want to spend
the rest of my life with.

—Cole.

The   Gap.

The gap feels a lot bigger than it actually is. It's just the small space between what we want and what we currently have.

The gap is the fear.

Sometimes it's divorce. Other times it's commitment. Sometimes it's starting the business. Other times it's doubling down on the career. Sometimes it's having the tough conversation. Other times it's keeping the tough conversation to one's self.

The gap is small.

No bigger than a foot wide. One step and we can stand on the other side. But, when most of us approach the gap, we look down. And, when we look down we see that it falls for miles and miles and miles.

Or, perhaps that's just the story we've been telling ourselves.

–Cole.

Hurt.

Sometimes,
I wonder if we hurt
others because we
feel lonely in our
own pain.

—Cole.

Scarecrow.

For most of the week they lurk deep in the abyss of my mind—only creeping to the forefront when the world slows down and it's distractions become non-existent. Staying busy keeps unhappy folks like myself from thinking about how unhappy we are. It's the busyness that keeps the unhappiness at bay. Covered up, quieted and disguised behind the drapes of ambition—momentarily out of sight but never out of mind.

When the world slows, the make-up begins to crack as the bells and whistles of life's demands aren't scare-crowing the thoughts away. This is when the mind begins to race.

Slowly at first then quickly then chaotically then unbearably—ever-faster with godspeed.

Godspeed.
Godspeed.
God, speed me into Monday.

Please.

—Cole.

Crushing.

I do wonder
if we ever
fully let go
of our
childhood crushes.

Perhaps not
the people
as much as the feelings
they gave us.

–Cole.

Tis the season.

I imagine
there are people hurting
right now
with the holidays nearing in.

Hurt, unfortunately, comes with the season.
I can't pretend to know your pain
but I can say sorry.

And,
I can give you a bit of advice
that has helped me
in times
when I have felt raw.

Be thankful for the hurt.

Find meaning in the hurt.

And,
understand every moment that it hurts
represents another moment
you're alive
and breathing
and living
and loving
and experiencing
all the beauty
this world has to offer.

–Cole.

48.

A novel idea.

She
said
she
wanted
to
live
forever,

I
said
she
should
fall
in
love
with
a
writer.

—Cole.

A few short rules worth living by:

1. Make good art.
2. Live fast.
3. Pet dogs.
4. Give without expectation.
5. Say nice things to others, daily.
6. Leave people better than you found them.
7. Buy experiences more often than products.
8. Always make time for coffee with people you care about.

–Cole.

Christmas night.

I do wonder why we all feel a bit lonely on the night of Christmas.

Perhaps it's because we're experiencing a comedown after the sensory overload of lovely faces and warm smiles and boisterous laughter and savory food and pretty things wrapped in pretty paper.

Regardless, I have yet to have a Christmas where the night of I'm not longing for a bottle of wine or a woman's touch or a cigarette or perhaps all three.

I'd argue the comedown is worth it, though.

−Cole.

Everywhere.

he asked her where it hurt,
she said

everywhere.

–Cole.

Curation.

They were lying naked on their
bellies floating between the
sheets in the calmness that
comes in waves after the storm
of lovemaking.
Talks that only happen on
pillows with pretty strangers
followed as their breaths grew light.
Some of these talks were small.
Some of them were big.
And, of the big ones,
a line stood out that she said to him
as her chin rested over crossed arms.
She said when people die,
they don't die as people
but rather a curation of their
life's loveliest moments
and she said she has never aspired
to be a person with a lot of years
but rather a curation of
lovely experiences.

—Cole.

Bravely you.

Inside each and
every one of us,
there is someone
we long to be.

I've always had
great admiration
for those brave enough
to be that person.

–Cole.

Fried Rice.

My grandmother was full-blooded Japanese, she was my best friend.
She lived right down the street from my parents' house.
After school when I got off the bus I would run to her front door.
She would sit me down at the kitchen table and make me a snack.
She would ask me about my day.
She would ask me what I learned.
She would tell me how much she loved me.
All while making me my favorite snack.
Fried rice.
Five years back, she dropped dead from a massive aneurysm.
She was standing in her kitchen when it happened.
Right by the kitchen table.
Right where she used to cook for me and ask me about my day.
And, tell me how much she loved me.
God took her there, of all places.
I still miss her.
Some days more than others.
And, no matter how hard I try.
The fried rice never quite tastes the same.
I don't think it ever well.

–Cole.

Let's play pretend.

He
        told
            her
                he
                    was
                        okay
                            with
                                pretending.

Pretending
        to
            be
                in
                    love
                        while
                            the
                                two
                                    of
                                        them
                                            waited
                                                for
                                                    l
                                                    o
                                                    v
                                                    e.

–Cole.

Why are you here?

The two most important days in your life are the day you are born and the day you find out why.

Mark Twain wrote that.

And, while I don't know a lot, what I do know is this…

We owe it to ourselves, the people we love, the people we've met, the people who aren't born yet and humanity as a whole to spend every ounce of our energy discovering the latter.

–Cole.

Claws.

Her scent was lovely,
with each passing breath
it pulled me in deeper,
digging its french manicured claws
into my chest and back
urging something primal in me
to lose control.

—Cole.

Whisky + Wine.

I used to panic when I got lonely.
I'd look for things and people and places to run to.
I still do that from time to time.
But that's normally after I grab one or two glasses of whisky or wine.
And, write something pretty about the loneliness.

–Cole.

Mastery.

Triumph is a rose never held
by the fiddler,
the finagler,
the hobbyist
and the tyre kicker.

It's a rose that only comes
to those who have the grit
to bite the goddamn bullet
and crack a few teeth—
those courageous enough
to stick their necks out
and commit years
(and in some cases light years)
to what they were put
on this Earth to do.

Triumph is a rose felt
and seen by a brave few—
a handful of renegades
willing to risk their lives,
their money,
their reputations,
their happiness
to cross the chasm— it has no patience
for the jack of all trades
(master of none).
It wants one thing and one thing only:

Mastery.

−Cole.

Talk to me.

I can tell you're hurting
by the way you're existing
in this room so noisily
without saying a single word.

−Cole.

Chasing the inferno.

Like the volcano or the Phoenix, the creative process is an inferno that makes room for something new, something brilliant, something lovely. It's messy. It's bloody. It's demanding. It's rigorous. But, it's also human. We destroy things not out of hatred but out of love—to make room to till the soil and plant the seeds of our vision. So, when you find yourself feeling self-destructive, don't panic. Instead, reflect.

What vision are you subconsciously making room for?

–Cole.

The chute.

He told her that it normally went away after a
few drinks, and he placed his finger on the spot
below the sternum, the spot that holds the chute
where a man's heart falls, when he's either falling
in love or losing someone he fell in love with.

−Cole.

Ass cheeks & Maseratis.

The moment we find ourselves feeling bored, sad, anxious or complacent we reach for our phones, a prescription or a self-help book. We've become terrified of feeling anything negative.

I'm not going to point a finger, but if someone held a gun to my head and told me to point a finger, I'd point to Instagram and Twitter and Facebook. I'd say we were due. I'd say that when you have an entire society overly focused on sharing the upper 1% of their days in a virtual world 24/7, we were bound to create some deep-rooted fears and insecurities around negative emotions. Now, we are forced to reap what we have sown.

Today, young men and women are so obsessed with not feeling boredom, sadness, anxiousness and complacency (or essentially the normal emotions of life) that they look to create a virtual world where they're living in that upper 1% all the time.

One where someone is eating avocado toast while drinking a mojito on a beach with a MacBook and a wad of cash in their lap and a sandy pair of ass cheeks next to a Maserati in the background (even though a Maserati doesn't belong on a beach) all of which is picture perfectly highlighted by a beautiful sunset.

The cost?

They're not really living. It's a facade. It looks pretty. It keeps out the bad. But it hides a plastic unpleasant reality.

–Cole.

Crimson T.

To live fully is to have the courage
to make the uncomfortable
decision of not playing it small—
even when not playing it small
means you'll be limping home
with nothing but a jacked jaw,
busted eye and a crimson t-shirt to
show for your moment of
lion-heartedness.

–Cole.

Dead rabbits & deader spirits.

The creative that survives strictly off her creativity has one of the toughest jobs in the world. Every morning she laces up her boots and ties them taut, she bundles up to break the cold and she grabs her spear like a lifeline as she sets out to find her next kill. But, for her, success isn't measured by the kill. Yes, it feeds her but it does not nourish her. No, for the creative, success is measured by the work. The days she leaves everything out in the wilderness and trudges back empty-handed are the days she feels full. Her stomach might hiss and growl as she goes to bed hungry. But her spirit rests easy knowing she did the work. However, the days she grab-asses, gets lucky, spears a rabbit, are the days she feels hungrier and emptier than ever before. Sure, her stomach keeps mum. But she tosses and turns long into the night as she is plagued and nightmared by the truth—the truth that she did not do the work. The creative does not live off wins. The creative lives off the work. That's what keeps her nourished.

—Cole.

One through seven.

This is a pretty story
that never happened.

–Cole.

One.

He was outside smoking a cigarette,
trying like hell to muffle the pain in his chest,
when she walked by,
an angel in the dark,
with a pair of red Converses
she wore like Christian Louboutins.

–Cole.

Two.

When the two of them locked eyes,
he ashed his cigarette
afraid she thought lowly of smoking
and because he had just found new addiction
and pain relief
in her technicolor eyes.

—Cole.

Three.

He was intimidated,
but her perfume dragged him in
after her
where he casually,
or not so casually,
found a place next to her at a knuckle-worn bar.

−Cole.

Four.

Smoking would one day kill him,
but in that moment it saved his life;
nicotine-cooled nerves gave him the courage
to ask her her name
and her drink of choice,
she said wine,
something red.

–*Cole.*

Five.

After a few glasses,
they determined they were both broken glasses,
hurting and lonely and a bit out of sorts,
and decided it'd be best
if they spent the rest of the night together at his place
where the wine selection was better,
so they stepped outside onto the street,
dodging a puddle
that reflected a moon so big
it looked like it could fall out of the sky.
They both acted like they were cold,
looking for an excuse to lean into one another.

–Cole.

Six.

The scent of her quickly
became the centerpiece of the speeding cab,
muffling out the smell of incense
and leftover Chinese food.
For a moment,
he thought he was falling in love
as the passing street lights lit up her angel-face
like Christmas morning.

–Cole.

Seven.

They stumbled into his flat
at the edge of town,
they drank more (red) wine
and fucked each other's minds for a good while
exploring all sorts of painful topics
one can only explore with strangers
one will never see again.
After the talking moved to whispering
and cooing
and kissing,
they fell quiet
and licked each other's wounds.

–Cole.

Too emotional.

Growing up I used to get made fun of
for being too emotional.
I remember one time
walking home from middle school crying
because a girl I was crushing on
called me gay
for being too emotional.
I remember it all hurt like hell.
I remember being held
by my momma that afternoon
for being too emotional.
And, I remember she said people
would one day appreciate me
for being too emotional.
Looking back it's all very ironic because
I grew up and found a pen.
Now I make six-figures a year
for being too emotional.
I get flown across the world
for being too emotional.
Women think I'm attractive
for being too emotional.
And, that last bit is shitty,
and angsty,
and petty
and arrogant.
But, it's not my fault.

I'm too emotional.

—Cole.

75.

Living with strained bones.

For a long time,
I feared death.

I feared waking up in another world,
or on the contrary,
not waking up at all.

But I no longer fear death.

I do, however, fear life.

I fear a life unlived.

To put it in another's words
far more poetic than my own,
Jonathan Safran Foer once wrote,

*"Sometimes I can hear my bones straining
under the weight of all the lives I'm not living."*

While I don't fear my bones being buried,
I do fear living with strained ones.

—Cole.

Happiness formula.

I don't know the secret to happiness. But, I know these things can't hurt. Shooting nerf guns. Flying to places you've never been. Playing ukulele. Getting high and cooking. Eating frozen pizza at 3 a.m., inebriated. Reading books. Dreaming of one day writing books. Eating cleaner (save for frozen pizza at 3 a.m.) Taking pictures of lovely things. Listening to Frank Ocean. Listening to Cigarettes After Sex. Listening to Bon Iver. Sipping coffee with people you care about. Dedicating moments each day to being grateful you're alive and breathing. Doing drugs on occasion (responsibly). Challenging your body and mind with strenuous exercise. Telling people you love, you love them. Lying in bed naked with pretty people. Petting dogs. Giving fewer fucks about what others think of you. Stacking money like a fucking G. Spending said stacked money on extraordinary experiences. Tipping your waiters and waitresses handsomely. Watching and being extraordinarily proud of your brother's success. Worrying less about a tomorrow that you're not promised. Taking yourself and others less seriously. Attending live music. Soaking in hot tubs with close friends. Building businesses. Making good art. Making good art. Making good art. Trying like hell to leave the world a little better than you found it.

–Cole.

Black & Blue.

& i have mixed emotions
about prostitution
but i'd pay
to run my fingers
through your hair
for an afternoon.

& i like my face intact
but i'd let your boyfriend
turn it black and blue
if i could kiss all over yours.

& i'm scared of heights
and far away frozen places
but i'd climb mountains
in the snow
if it meant i could
walk you home.

–Cole.

To Holly, forever ago.

If I could, I would reach accross the screen and grab you and probably kiss you and tell you to quiet that voice inside your head that's keeping you from making the brilliant fucking art you're capable of. If I could, I would give you a glimpse into the future — a future where you're art is worn by everyone, everywhere. If I could, I would give you that gift. But, I can't. So, you're just gonna have to close your eyes and take my word for it — and I hope to God you do — because this world will be a hell of a lot prettier if you do. In fact, I think that's why you're here, love. To pretty things up before you leave.

But, I digress.

–Cole.

Living hurt.

It's no longer a question of

"if"

this life is going to hurt you.

It will always hurt you

no matter what you do.

Hurt comes with the territory of living.

The question must become

what is worth the hurt.

We must determine

what is worth hurting for.

—Cole.

Champagne.

For a long time, I thought it was
money that would make me
happy. Now that I have more than
I know what to do with, I'm
realizing I was right. I like picking
up the tab at dinner for people I
love and I like buying nerf guns and
I like flying where I want when
I want and I like giving my waitress a
$100 tip because the universe
tells me she's going through hell.

It's wildly popular to believe
money is the root of all evil and
that it can't buy happiness and that
it is wrong to want more and that
we should be ashamed of it. But,
I'm not drinking that Kool-aid.

I prefer champagne.

−Cole.

Acrylic.

She traced the edges of my tattoos
with her black acrylics
like she was etching them
into my skin for the first time.

We both made each other feel good
but we didn't expect it to last forever.

I'm not sure we wanted it to.

Eventually,
like her nails,
we'd outgrow one another
and want for something more.

There was a finite
sort of acrylic beauty in it all.

Or, at least I like to think so.

–Cole.

Fireflies.

i wanted like hell to catch her gaze,
but doing so felt like moving mountains,
pulling those pretty technicolor eyes my way
was like treading water in steel toe boots,
i chased them long and hard,
i chased them until i was out of breath,
i chased them like those Indiana fireflies,
i used to catch as a kid.

(her eyes were much faster, though).

−Cole.

Dear, Steinbeck.

I ran into an old acquaintance the other night. He looked mostly good but I could tell he was hurting from heartbreak. There's a sort of emptiness in the eyes that lingers for a while after someone who meant the world to you, leaves. That emptiness was there, behind it all.

Over the years I have found bars to be poor places to help old friends piece together the brokeness. Normally the drunkenness of it all washes the conversation from memory in the morning or makes the conversation subpar at best.

But, if he is reading this right now, I would like to share with him one of my favorite lines from one of my favorite writers, John Steinbeck. The writer's son was once struggling with heartbreak and what Steinbeck told his son was something simple yet lovely.

He said, *"Nothing good gets away."*

−Cole.

It's cyclical.

Most of the creative's pain is self-inflicted.

He creates his own destruction and he destroys his own creations.

He rubs honey on his gaping wounds to pretend that they're not there.

He creates to cover up what's coming undone.

He writes in hopes the ink will cover up the tracks of his tears.

He creates to take away the pain he has created.

It's cyclical.

–Cole.

Chest.

There's little room for rationality in love. There's room for compassion, honesty and forgiveness. But, if you're approaching love with a sense of rationality, like it's some black and white problem to be solved, you're not truly loving. You might think you're loving. But you're not truly loving.

We live in a society where people are rewarded on how "rational" they can be, they are praised on their ability to remove their hearts and their emotions from their thinking and make calculated decisions based on fact.

To each their own, but I'm not going to fuck with these people nor am I going to fuck these people. I'm here for a short time and if you're going to love me (be it as a friend or as a lover) you better set your fucking heart on the table. You better be loving me hard and recklessly with that big beating organ in your chest.

Or, just don't love me at all.

–Cole.

Broken pieces.

They both showed up to the party
with handfuls of their broken pieces
in hopes that one another
would be a distraction
from their broken pieces
and for a while,
the fucking was a wonderful distraction.

Until it wasn't.

Until the fucking transformed into feelings
(as fucking has a way of doing)
and the two of them found themselves
trying to piece one another back together again
because they felt strongly
about making one another whole.

It all got very messy and bloody.

Some of the broken pieces were quite sharp
and some of the broken pieces
ended up in the other's pile of broken pieces.

It was all quite tragic.

–Cole.

It's funny.

Love is funny.

Sometimes we know it when we see it.

Sometimes we see it and we don't know it for a while.

Sometimes we feel it and the other person doesn't.

Sometimes we fake it to get over the love we have for someone else.

Love is funny and at times beautiful and at times painful.

And, at times so much of the latter…

we
swear
we'll
never
do
it
again.

Yet we always do.

Love is so funny in this way.

–Cole

Don't dip your toes in.

I was born in a small town in southern indiana nestled by a river you were told not to dip your toes in.

Up close the river left something to be desired, but if you walked beside it on a summer night with the moon shining just right you'd swear it was the prettiest place on earth.

In my town, there were dreamers and there were lovers. The dreamers wanted to run away to far away places, while the lovers wanted to stay put and make love and babies and families.

The river had a way of causing a lot of trouble for the dreamers and the lovers. When they'd walk hand in hand alongside the moonlit river on a summer night, something magically troublesome would happen.

They'd fall in love.

—Cole.

Looking.

You're not looking at her.
You're looking at tomorrow.
You're looking at your dreams.
You're looking at far away places.
You're looking over the fence at greener grasses.
You're looking everywhere but there.
Right there in front of you.
And, I think you're going to regret it.
Because I've seen a lot of people looking.

And, I have never seen anyone look at someone the way she looks at you.

—*Cole.*

Of Gods and men.

Women are gods. Or, goddesses
rather. They can crumble entire
empires with a whisper. They can
drop a man to his knees with the
batting of an eye. They can create
life. They can nourish it. They can
sculpt it into something that might
go on to change humanity forever.
Those who create us aren't people.
They aren't like us men. They
aren't equal. They are far greater.
They walk among us with these
beautiful brains and big beating
hearts housed inside a body
festooned with long thick hair,
pouty lips, sun-kissed skin, blazing
green eyes and pillowy breasts.
They're goddesses willing to give
us everything, all of themselves,
and all they ask in return is to be
worshipped.

–Cole.

91.

10,000

I've been living with reckless abandon lately. I'm slinging 10,000 words a week. I'm tearing through books like they're vintage porn magazines. I'm hitting the hot yoga studio, flirting with suicide by heat exhaustion. I'm knifing my way through the sky in big jet planes to see pretty people in pretty places. I'm dreaming of empires like I've got Rockefeller blood racing through my veins.

I'm losing my fucking mind at dimly lit bars where the bass drowns out my thoughts and weighs heavily against my chest like CPR.

I'm spiraling. I'm losing control.

Here soon I'm going to come skidding through the finish line battered and bloody.

—Cole.

Half-assing vulnerability.

Most vulnerability we see today
isn't true vulnerability.
It's convenient vulnerability.
It's being vulnerable to better one's
position in the public eye.
It's conditional vulnerability.
It's this idea that one will only be
vulnerable in situations where it's
advantageous to one's self.
Being vulnerable should be a selfless act.
It's making the difficult choice of sharing the
raw painful truth in hopes to build
something beautiful from that suffering.

–Cole.

Shy or something.

I am deeply shy and terribly
insecure.

Often times this gets mistaken for
arrogance because I have a pretty
face and shy insecure pretty-faced
people can easily be assumed
arrogant.

I don't know, maybe I am a little
arrogant. But I'm shy too. And,
definitely insecure. You should
feed me wine and kiss on my neck
and tell me I'm easy on the eyes
because I'm deeply shy and
terribly insecure and perhaps a bit
arrogant and those lips of yours
look like they could send shivers
down my spine.

—Cole.

Fahrenheit 451.

I've got a big beautiful pair of waxwings on my back.
You should see the way they flap.
When they get going, when they really get to flapping, I can fly.

I fly higher and higher and higher until I'm so close to the sun my wings melt. And, hot wax sets my back on fire and I begin to fall, fall, fall.

When I finally come crashing into the ground like a fallen angel or one of those glowing meteors that look like indigo fireballs in the sky — I can't breath.

But, I like not breathing as much as I like flying.
I like falling as much as I like shooting for the sun.

I like the feeling of hot wax running down my back as much as I like my wings.

I like to burn.

–Cole.

Life is a banshee worth loving.

When we're hurting we must remind ourselves that there is beauty in the pain. Jamming our bare toes on the jutted barstool is a nice colorful reminder that we're still human. That we can still feel. That we're still here… living… breathing… existing. The same can be said for massive failures, heartbreaks and lost loved ones. They are screaming biting clawing banshees that haunt us. But they are banshees worth loving nonetheless because they remind us that we're still alive.

–Cole.

Molly.

I'm not addicted to drugs nor
alcohol. But I'm addicted to
the moments that come with
them, like watching your
technicolor eyes glow like
a pair of UFO's under
dancing lights as you lift
up your hair with your matte
black fingernails, getting
lost in the songs that were
written for your soul. In
these moments the room
is flipped on its head as we
float through space in
zero-gravity, your hair
racing skyward as if God
spun Angel Falls upside
down to shower heaven
and the clouds and the
angels and himself in its vastness.

—Cole.

Play it big or die trying.

I'm not here for a long time. I've
never seen myself growing old and if manifestation
holds true like it has all my life,
the reaper will come and
claim me before I have too many grays sprouting
from my head. I've told myself
I'd bite the dust young for
a while now. In part because I'm a deranged
romantic who believes there's a beauty
in going out while still climbing the mountain.
But, mostly because it provides
me with a sense of urgency.
I don't have all the time
in the world to change the world
(or at the very least, the little bit of world around me),
so I better bite bullets, swallow fire,
pull no punches and sling ink like each
word is adding a few more ounces
of sand to my hourglass. I better play it big
every goddamn second of every goddamn day.
I better play it big or die trying.
I sure would love to die trying,
to die a warrior-poets death.
Mid-sentence, no period
and with a thought left
unfinished.

—Cole.

Universe.

I don't care what you do when I'm not around. Scratch that.
I do care.
I care about you doing everything.
I want you to do and experience everything. Hunt dreams.
Love friends.
Kiss strangers.
Climb mountains.
See places.
Devour moments.
Grow lightyears.
Do everything your heart desires.
And, then some.
You were meant to use your wings.
All that I ask is when we cross paths.
During the tiny precious moments we'll find.
I'm the center of your universe.

—*Cole.*

Stop Loitering.

Loitering is when you stand or
wait around with no apparent purpose.
It sounds ridiculous, but it's a common occurrence,
so common that many gas stations and restaurants
will post signs stating No Loitering.
To the onlooker who doesn't spend
their time loitering outside
McDonald's the act might seem ridiculous.
However, many of us are loitering in
our lives, careers, and relationships.
We're waiting around with
no apparent purpose.

—Cole.

My space girl.

The sun had just fallen below the horizon and
the night was becoming night and we were both
tipsy, her off wine and I off her. She pointed up
to the vast dark blue space between several stars
in the sky and she said it was her favorite color
and I think in that moment it became
my favorite color, too.

−Cole.

Tyson.

Mike Tyson once said,

*"The tempt for greatness is the biggest
drug in the world."*

That has always resonated with me
and I imagine it resonates with any
young ambitious individual crazy
enough to believe they can take on
the world.

The idea of not becoming great at what
I do keeps me up at night.
It's an addiction. It's a drug.

And, like any drug, the addict must
eventually decide whether
the high is worth it.

I've lost friends, love and, to be honest,
a part of myself chasing
the high of greatness—

*even as I write this right now I'm
thinking about my next hit.*

—Cole.

Surgery.

Her problem was
that she kept
showing up to
relationships still
battered and
bloody from
previous ones,
expecting her new
lovers to provide
the healing she
needed, but they
weren't surgeons,
they were
accountants and
semi-pro athletes
and bartenders and
fitness instructors

but not surgeons.

—Cole.

Fuck me I'm lying.

The reason most people struggle to be honest with other people is because they struggle to be honest with themselves. The scariest demon in the world to face is our own authentic selves. The truth we see at night when our heads hit our pillows, or on Sundays when the world is too slow to distract us from our own thoughts. It's in these vulnerable moments that we string together brilliant fabricated lies in the form of stories in hopes to escape our truths. And, what's worse is that the stories work. We're able to lie to ourselves without realizing we're lying to ourselves. Much of our lives are fiction. Fiction of our own creation.

—Cole.

House of red balloons.

I walked in. I handed the hostess at the bar three balloons I had stolen from a previous bar. I asked her to look after them for me. Just for a little while — while I danced the night away. She said yes. She had tattoos. I told her I liked them. She smiled but didn't say thank you. I danced for a good while under the blue lights with a best friend of mine named Robert. He is also a writer. In between blaring songs, we stepped outside and smoked a cigarette. I only smoke cigarettes when I'm drunk. It's a bad habit. But, they make me feel cool like James Dean. Some might call them an affectation, like the red balloons. I'm not so sure. Robert eventually found a cute girl to dance with. I went and found the hostess looking after my balloons because I needed company. She handed them to me. They were neatly tied together. I stepped outside and let them go. They floated until they got caught on an electrical line. They danced there for a while in the wind. Under the great big stars that were asking them to let go.

—Cole.

Love is not clipping wings.

We often confuse love with possession.
Unlike our pets, humans weren't meant to be kept on leashes.
They weren't meant to be neutered and spayed.
Their wings weren't meant to be clipped for the sake of your possession.
When you love someone, you love them unconditionally.
You love them not under the condition they'll be here forever.
But, rather, that they chose to be here, for a moment or a lifetime.
Even though they could have flown anywhere.

–Cole.

Runner/ Runner.

When she and I approached the
finish line we were both exhausted.
We did it to ourselves.
We chose to run the race.
It was beautiful most of the time.
Except for the times it wasn't.
And, I think we could have kept running.
I really do. I imagine we're still the same people.
I imagine we could do it all again.
But, it wouldn't be the same.
You know how running goes.
After you decide to stop and take a break,
you can start again but you'll never run for long.
It just doesn't feel the same.
I think we make the mistake of revisiting
past lovers because we miss the feelings
they gave us (not necessarily the people).
We miss the race. We miss the runner's high
we shared together. I still run, just alone now,
sometimes this gets me high.
When it doesn't and I really need to feel
something I'll smoke and watch
a documentary about cancer or tear through
a pack of cherry flavored cigarettes on a
Tuesday night, or get all sorts of fucked up
and run my fingers through a stranger's hair.
You'd be surprised how many strangers
like getting their hair played with.
I think most of them are running too.

–Cole.

107.

Stranger than fiction.

Falling for people through screens is dangerous. It's fiction. It's stranger than fiction. We're not falling for people, but rather the idea of them we've fabricated in our own heads. It's like falling in love with Lady Brett Ashley in Hemingway's The Sun Also Rises. After I read Hemingway, I fell in love with that woman. But, I can't take her to dinner because she doesn't exist. And, that is our generation's curse, falling for the pretty fiction behind glowing screens that we create in our own heads. At times, I wonder if our imaginations will be the death of any chance we have at love.

−Cole.

Tremors.

When I was in Belarus my hair grew long and I needed it cut, so I went roaming the streets in search of a barber, something easier said than done when you can't read Russian. Eventually, I happened upon this hair salon in a basement under a fast food restaurant. I walked in and there were four women in there. They stared wide-eyed, like they had never seen a mutt like me before. I motioned to my head and said I needed a buzz cut. They laughed because they didn't speak English. Finally, a pretty older lady grabbed me by my arm and took me to a chair. She began shaving my head with a pair of old clippers. Her hands, her wrists, her face and her neck were shaking softly but steadily. At first, I thought she was laughing but she wasn't. She was suffering from tremors. Parkison's, perhaps. I watched her as she shook and I watched as she was doing everything she could not to shake. But, despite the shaking, she willed herself to hold the clippers steady. She gave me a splendid haircut. When I left I tried to give her $25, which is what I pay my barber back home. She wouldn't take it because the price was $5. I asked her again and again. She wouldn't. I'm not sure if it was her pride, but she had a dedication to her craft like I had never seen before. I hope I write like she cuts when I'm her age. That, or I hope I'm dead.

—Cole.

To the kids that were hurt.

Everyone reading this right now is suffering from childhood trauma. You might not be aware of it but it's in there, hiding.

The impact is massive on how you view yourself, others, the world, your work and your relationships.

Sometimes this trauma is severe. Maybe you were abused sexually, physically or emotionally by an adult.

Other times, this trauma is more subtle. Maybe your parent, teacher or coach was overly critical of you. Maybe you constantly felt like you were living in a sibling's shadow. Maybe you were made fun of by other boys and girls.

Regardless of what your trauma is, it's imperative that you confront it, head on.

Eventually, you must find the courage to say, "I've been acting in the following way because of something that happened in my childhood that was completely out of my control. I deserve to be free of that trauma."

As you confront your own trauma, remember that like you and I, most of the hateful humans we run into on a daily basis are just grown-up children, hurting. That's heartbreaking. But it's freeing. It gives us permission to be better to ourselves and our fellow humans.

–Cole.

Black Valentine.

please – love today like you're running out of time.

–*Cole.*

Let her keep her wings.

I struggled with jealousy for a long time, especially in relationships.

As I grew to understand myself on a deeper level, I realized this jealousy was just the tip of a much larger iceberg I was ignoring below the surface. I was battling a horrible fear of abandonment. I was jealous of other men where it concerned the women I was dating because I was scared of losing her to him. I was at war. Love should be many things but it should never be war. Jealousy was my body and mind's way of doing everything I could to not be abandoned, to not feel that pain of someone leaving. As a result, I led an exhausting life. I couldn't enjoy love or intimacy because I was so fucking terrified of losing it. Numerous people, both men and women alike, struggle with jealousy. We attempt to mask it in our relationships as being healthy or flattering, branding it as some sort of fucked up proof our partners care about us. But jealousy is not love. It's selfishness. If we're not careful, it's an emotion that can quickly transform into possession.

Let her keep wings.

—Cole.

Off-pink.

Did you see the sunrise this morning?
The jet planes were kicking up snow like dust,
on the runway,
smoldering out the glow of the sun.
It painted the sky this lovely off-pink
like a faded rose.
I wanted to pick it for you,
as I floated past it through the sky.
But I couldn't.
I'm not sure if they make summer dresses that color,
nor if you wear summer dresses,
but that sunrise would look pretty on you.

−Cole.

113.

I've been on a roll since you last saw me.

Before one of my best friends got religious on me the two of us rolled molly and hopped on a giant Ferris Wheel in Chicago.

It's one of my favorite memories of all time.

It's weird because I think a part of him wants to forget it and a part of me wants to remember it forever and ever.

I think there is a metaphor for life hidden somewhere in there, but I'm still trying to figure it out.

−Cole.

Saint Valentine.

I love Conner for being a big brother to so many boys that have needed one. I love Trey for realizing he was put on this Earth to do the most important thing anyone can do. Create music. I love that blue-eyed girl in Belarus for smiling at me during a time I needed it most. I love Taylor for making every single person he runs into feel like they're the only person in the world that matters. I love Grace for showing up every single day, reminding the humans in this world that their bodies, minds and spirits are works of art that should be cherished. I love Luke for walking through hell and arising on the other side like a phoenix destined to set the world on fire. I love my dad for all the times he woke up while the sun was still sleeping to put food on the table; for teaching me what it means to be a warrior. I love my mother for loving fiercely, for raising three little banshees all the while killing it in her career. I love Auston for being quite possibly the most loving and loyal friend I will ever know. I love my third grade teacher, Mrs. Woodall, for making a broken insecure little boy feel like he could take over the world. I love Ian for his beautiful mind, for choosing to exist in the gray space, for his uncanny level of emotional empathy that the rest of us can only one day hope to achieve. I love my Meme for having the courage to cross the sea, to create a life in a foreign place (I have so much to tell you).

–Cole.

Demigod.

Eventually, all of us must come to
find that we ourselves are enough.
Reassurance and outside validation
are like drugs to the addict. They
feel good, at times even lovely. But
no hit will ever be enough.

I've met countless beautifully talented people
bursting at the seams with endless potential.

When I look at them I see queens
and kings, queendoms and kingdoms within arm's reach. I see
these demigods with all the power
in the world, yet they remain slaves to outside reassurance and
validation.

If no one has ever told you, please allow me to.

You are more powerful than you think you are.

You are more powerful than you think you are.

Yet, me saying it and even repeating it doesn't matter because that belief
needs to come from within, deep down in that cold place behind and
below your heart where they say your soul lies.

You need to know your greatness and eventually,
you need to know that you knowing it will forever be
enough.

—Cole.

From their falling.

It's pretty outside and
so are you and I'm not
sure if you saw but the
stars are so big tonight
they look like they're
going to fall out of the
sky, so I think it might
be best that we spend
the night together on
this blanket atop this wet
grass, I want to be there,
after all, to protect you
from their falling.

–Cole.

Flat White.

I keep buying flat whites from this pretty
blue-eyed Belarusian girl here in Minsk. She
doesn't speak English and I don't speak
Belarusian. But she smiles at me a lot and waves
goodbye when I exit through the back door and
onto the city's cold hard streets. Nothing will
come of it because nothing should, but she has
made my stay here, in the last dictatorship of
Europe, warmer. She has reminded me to smile and
wave more, especially to strangers and I'm
deeply thankful for her (and this reminder) even
though she keeps messing up my order.

—Cole.

Eyewater.

You've got running mascara
racing down your face
like bleeding novels.

—Cole.

33 God.

I'm still looking for God. Sometimes I'll catch a glimpse of him or her making a run for it far off in the distance, but we have yet to have a conversation.

I'm thankful, though. For him or her. I think he might be a she.

I'm thankful for her because she made sure my grandmother left me one last voicemail before she made her *French exit.*

I'm thankful for her because she made sure my parents found their way back to one another after they had gotten lost.

I'm thankful for her because she made sure I was okay, regardless of all those nasty things that happened to me as a child, so many times in that bathroom with the hideous green wallpaper, so long ago.

I'm thankful for her because she has always made sure I stumble upon the words when my writer's block kicks in and a deadline is due.

If I ever meet God, I'll be sure to buy her a drink.

I wonder if she drinks her wine red or white.

–Cole.

Black Magic.

Black roses lay scattered across the bathroom floor.

Cigarette ashes, crimson-painted wine corks and articles of clothing fill up the white space between them.

They're in the bathtub.

She's laughing uncontrollably, wine drunk and infatuated.

Blood trickling down his chin like racing horses.

He slipped a stem between his teeth to spark a smile on her pretty face, but a thorn put a tear in his lip the size of Manhattan.

She's laughing.

But now she's climbing on top of him, whispering in his ear about knowing something that'll make the pain go away.

—Cole.

Devour this moment whole.

For many years I spent my days dreaming and longing of future days with picket fences. It was a cancerous way of living and one that cost me years of my life as I continuously obsessed over tomorrow. I suppose as I've grown older, I've become very aware of my own mortality, realizing I'm just a speeding car or a doctor's call away from it all being over. This realization has changed everything for me. It has given me permission to devour each of life's moments whole. While I know you and I are different people in what feels like totally different worlds, I encourage you to live this same way. When you live with the understanding that each moment might be your last, everything changes. You begin loving the people in your life harder. You begin sacrificing your body and soul to make good work. You begin living with an insatiable appetite to devour the moment you're living in now. It will feel foreign but it will ignite your being. Death will no longer scare you as you come to the profound realization that the only death you truly face is not living fully now. So, please. I beg you. Devour this moment whole, my friend.

–Cole.

Addict.

I'm addicted to black and white photographs of
 celebrities smoking cigarettes.

I'm addicted to rainfall at bedtime.
I'm addicted to whispers that smell of vodka and cranberry.
I'm addicted to Moscow Mules in copper mugs and puffing cheap cigars.
I'm addicted to my late grandmama's Japanese accent (I miss you).
I'm addicted to pretty girls with tattoos and pretty girls without them.

I'm addicted to Hemingway and his closing line —
isn't it pretty to think so?

I'm addicted to living and dying and finding meaning in both.
I'm addicted to the silences in conversations;

the silent conversations.

–Cole.

Room to explore.

I do think it would be beneficial as a society if we practiced a freer form of love. Not necessarily openly fucking everything with reckless abandon. But, rather, allowing our partners to explore themselves and the world around them more fiercely. Love, as I see it today, is very conditional. It's this idea that as long as our partners fit within a specific set of conditions, constructs and expectations, we will continue to love them. That's a bit fucked up in my opinion. I think we need to give our partners room to explore, to make mistakes, to grow and to experience this life to the fullest. I think we need to remember that we are lovers, not keepers.

–Cole.

You're a dreamer.

May your dreams and ambitions
fly you to the moon and let you play
among the stars. May they drive you
to drink too much from time to time
in both celebration and at times in
disappointment. May they be big and
monstrous and lovely and may they
scare you and terrify you to the point
of greatness. May your dreams and
ambitions show you what it means
to be human—to be born into this
world for just long enough to leave
it better than you found it. If I wish
anything for you it's to dream and to
ambitiously chase those dreams with a
vengeance, forever and for a lifetime.

—Cole.

Two wrongs.

I have had my heart broken plenty of times,
and I have broken plenty of hearts too,
and I hope the hearts I've broken can forgive me,
for I have forgiven those that have broken mine.

–Cole.

Jesus.

Jesus showed up in front of my
Airbnb driving a pearl white
Dodge Town & Country. I got in
and before I could buckle up, he
told me he was getting the fuck out
of Denver, Colorado. I asked why.
He shook his head. *I asked
why again.* He shook his head again.

I then started to say that it wasn't
such a bad place and that the girls
were pretty. But, before I could
finish, he cut me off. He said all the
women here are cougars and that
they want puppy dogs, not wolves.

I laughed and said that I couldn't agree or disagree.
I then asked if I could steal that line. He said he didn't give a fuck.
He was in his late fifties. He was hispanic.
He had a face like a Taiwanese kick-boxer.

And, for the next fifteen minutes.
I listened to him bitch and there really wasn't anything interesting said,
except for that goddamn line that's making me write this piece right
now… they want puppy dogs, not wolves.

That's a damn pretty line. Anyway, Jesus is moving to Tampa in May
because it's hot, has a low cost of living and the
woman apparently like wolves down there.

—Cole.

127.

Undisturbed.

When it all comes crashing down,
it's the bits and pieces that will fuck you to pieces.
It's finding a strand of her hair on your pillowcase.
It's grabbing for the wrong toothbrush.
It's scrolling through the Spotify playlist that was made just for you.
It's getting your toes smashed by her falling shampoo.
I don't know why they make those fucking things so goddamn big.
It's discovering all her articles of clothing that went missing in action.
It's feeling your feet brush against yet another one of her hair ties.
It's searching for the courage to toss the red lipstick stained coffee cup

(sitting on the nightstand, undisturbed, like nothing ever happened)
(like she's going to walk right in and take another sip).

—Cole.

Chocolate milk, a latte and a mother fucking cookie.

I was sitting at my favorite coffee
shop this morning, banging my
head against my laptop in hopes that some words
would trickle out. Nothing did for a good while.
In fact, I was moments away from giving up
when in walked a chubby seven-year-old boy with a
Spiderman wallet. He approached the barista and
spouted off his order like he was giving a command
to his troops, "I want a
chocolate milk, a latte
and a cookie. Please."

I burst out laughing and so did
the woman next to me and the boy mean
mugged the two of us across the counter until her
and I both stopped. She and I then whispered
and snickered to one another about how
fucking prolific it was that this kid made his
order of chocolate milk, a latte and a cookie like a badass.

I'm not sure where the kid's parents were.
Honestly, it wouldn't surprise me if the little
punk played hooky from school and took a taxi.
All I know is that I need to command life
the way this little boy commands
his baristas and if I had a little girl
I wouldn't let her anywhere near him.

—Cole.

129.

Don't let go.

There will be moments in your life
when you stumble into someone and your whole
damn world will be flipped on its head, a complete stranger
will become the only person that matters and if I can
give you any piece of advice, it's that in
these moments don't let go.

—Cole.

Bald Eagle.

One of the best things I ever did was shave my head.

For a long time, I'd spend more time than I'd like to admit looking at myself in the mirror, analyzing where the strands fell, admiring how it looked, worrying over whether or not I'd one day lose it.

But then I shaved it.

And, when I shaved it, something changed, immediately.

I stopped worrying so much about what I saw in the mirror and I started focusing on the brain behind the hair, behind the ears, behind the face.

I started reading more and thinking more and creating more.

I'm sure it all sounds silly...

Today, I no longer worry about being the best looking guy in the room.

I want to be the smartest.
I want to be the most creative.
I want to be the most thoughtful.
I want to be the most interesting.

But, I couldn't give a shit less about being the best looking.

I want to be everything I wasn't born to be.

I want to be everything I've worked like hell to build.

—Cole

Pillow Therapy.

Most of men's problems stem from lack of non-sexual intimacy with their partners and perhaps a much deeper underlying fear of vulnerability. We've been socially conditioned to believe that having sex makes us more masculine and expressing vulnerability makes us weak. As a result, we live in a culture where men won't go to therapy. They will instead attempt to fuck the pain away, be it to a screen or with another human being. I've known great troubles, both mentally and emotionally, and many of them have been cured sitting alone in a room with a therapist. And, I'd argue just as many, if not more, have been cured spending fifteen to twenty minutes with my head on a woman's chest.

Fucking is good. But it's not medicine.

–Cole.

Rain.

Her
hair
was
thick
and
it
fell
forever,

it

reminded

me

of

pounding

rain.

–Cole.

This one fucked me up to write.

She and I didn't end in a horrible derailing crushing wreck that left both of us bloody and grabbing for our throats to check if we were still breathing—it was more like a slow dance.

We were holding each other closely, swaying to Cigarettes After Sex and I decided to gently let go of her hand and she didn't make the slightest attempt to grab it back.

And, in a cynical yet poetic way, this is what loving in a broken generation haunted by dreams feels like—a slow dance that gets *slower and slower until the music stops and someone lets go.*

—Cole.

(gone).

Forgotten love letters,
stowed away in old cigar boxes,
ink is fading,
but still legible
barely legible
then not legible at all

(gone)
(gone)
(gone)

collecting dust like childhood dreams.

—Cole.

Abandoning judgement.

Judgments are our own insecurities and fears reflected onto another person. Men judge highly successful women, labeling them bitches, because deep down they are terrified of the thought that their wives might one day be more successful than them. Women judge free-spirited promiscuous women, labeling them whores because deep down they are terrified they might one day find their husbands in bed with them. Racist white fathers judge black teenagers, labeling them a word I won't repeat because deep down they are terrified that their daughters might end up loving someone of a different skin tone. There is nothing good about judgment. Absolutely nothing. It can, however, be used as a tool to gain a better understanding of ourselves and our own insecurities. When you find yourself judging someone, take a step back. Ask yourself, *what deep underlying insecurity or fear is this person triggering in me?* During the most judgmental phases of my life, I was also extremely insecure and unhappy. I couldn't face my own insecurities and unhappiness so instead, I chose to reflect these feelings onto others in the form of judgment. Today, when I feel myself becoming judgmental towards anyone, it serves as a nice reminder that
I have some internal work to do
and I do it.

—Cole

The time I thought I pissed my pants.

The first time I ever smoked marijuana I got so paranoid that I thought I was actually pissing my pants for like an hour straight. Which might sound ridiculous to you but imagine being so high that you think you've lost complete control of your bladder in a social setting. It's kind of fucked up. Anyway, thankfully, I didn't actually piss my pants and after a few more tries became somewhat fond of the devil's lettuce.

–Cole.

Love is infinite.

We cannot, under any circumstance, hate our past loves. We can walk away. We can wish it had all turned out different. We can hurt. We can cry. We can smile. We can be relieved it's over. We can learn. Most importantly we can learn.

But we cannot, under any circumstance, hate them. Our past loves show us how to love and sometimes they show us how not to love. Regardless, we must be extraordinarily thankful for them.

Love is the only energy in this world that is infinite. The love you'll one day show your person isn't just your love. It's a collection or a cultivation, rather, of the love you were shown (be it good or bad) by those who came before him or her.

In this writer's fucked up head, that's one of the most beautiful aspects of being human and loving—that we can love someone fiercely and that they can then take the lessons and the feelings and the good and the bad of our love and repurpose it to love someone else, fuller.

–Cole.

Going bad.

I no longer want to be good.
I just want to be real.

I suppose it has taken me until now to realize they're
rarely one in the same.

$-Cole.$

To the pretty fearless girl in Warsaw.

I was in Warsaw.
My flight was running late.
Sitting across from me was a mother and daughter.
They looked to be exhausted. The three of us began talking.
The daughter was young, maybe twenty-two.
She had been interning abroad in Warsaw for a semester.
She told me her trip was cut short because she had suffered a minor stroke.
After being hospitalized for a week, she
was now stable and traveling home.
As I looked at them I noticed the fear in both their eyes.
I noticed the fear they were experiencing was quite
a bit different from one another. For the mother,
she was scared she was going to lose her daughter.
The daughter was scared she was going to lose the opportunity.
The opportunity to chase down her dreams of working abroad and
traveling the world. It was all very sad and lovely at the same time.
I think it was my first look into what it's like to be a parent.
All our lives we have these big dreams
and ambitions until we create new life.
Then, our dreams and ambitions become them.
The three of us talked for an hour.
I never got the daughters name and I wished I had because I would have
written to her. I'm telling myself that her being a
page in my book will be enough, though.
She's going to be alright and her mother will be too.
I'm quite certain of it. Even though she was tired, she
was also pretty and fearless and she had big dreams.
And, you can't kill pretty fearless girls with big dreams.
Those girls have a way of living forever.

—Cole.

140.

Summer.

Blazing through city streets
street lights passing like tracers,
like lightsabers on your pretty face,
you're glowing between the flashes
my heart is absorbing all the burn
and the marijuana is making the pounding music
feel like summer rain in my chest.

–Cole

Like, now.

Life is about rhythm and it's about momentum. It's not unlike writing in this way. Good writers craft their prose with rhythm and they use that rhythm to build momentum. Right now, you're reading this and we're dancing. Side to side. Just you and me. Feeling one another out with each passing sway. *That's rhythm.* But, eventually, something changes. I start to add some punch. Some oomph. Some vinegar. Some chutzpah. I grab you by the neck and drag you across the fucking page to keep up with me. To keep pace. That's momentum. You're more focused now. You're more alert. We're no longer dancing. We're fighting. In writing, rhythm makes the reader comfortable. Momentum moves them into action. If rhythm is *Beauty.* Momentum is *The Beast.* Life isn't unlike writing in this way. It must be equal parts rhythm and momentum. Equal parts *Beauty and The Beast.* You need rhythm to feel comfortable. But, to take action you need momentum. You need to grab yourself by the neck, step out the door and fucking sprint. You need to sprint. This is me telling you, you need to sprint. Like, now.

–Cole.

I'm scared.

I'm scared of long drives and being alone in my head.
I'm scared of the dentist picking at my teeth with that hook thing.
I'm scared of the plane when it shakes hard.

I'm scared of never getting to say goodbye to the
people who cared enough to read.

I'm scared of looking people in the eyes.
I'm scared of you never realizing how powerful you are.
I'm scared of not being all that I know I'm capable of being.
I'm scared of dying young.
I'm scared of living old.
I'm scared of talking to pretty girls.
I'm scared of my best friends getting hurt by pretty girls.
I'm scared of hurting pretty girls.
I'm scared of ghosts (the real ones and the ones we make up).

I'm scared of finding that one person I want
to spend the rest of my life with.

I'm scared of never finding that one person
I want to spend the rest of my life with.
I'm scared of people realizing how insecure I am.
I'm scared of falling in love with someone else
before falling in love with myself.

I'm scared of the money changing me.
I'm scared of the possibility that there is no heaven.
I'm scared of the possibility that there is one.

—Cole.

Jaguar.

Sad-eyed models in old black and white photographs,
smoking cigarettes on rusty New York fire escapes,
high-heels dangling seven stories up,
fur coats covering goose-bumped skin.

–Cole.

Let's swing.

When I was a little boy I had a crush on this little girl.
She liked to swing.
I liked to swing because she liked to swing.
I would always jump on a swing three swings from hers.
Close but not too close.
Close enough to look at how pretty she was.
But not so close that she'd know I liked her.

I slowly built up the courage to swing two swings away from her.
Then one swing away from her.
Until one day, I decided it was time to swing next to her.
I walked up to her while she was swinging.
I asked her if anyone was swinging there.
I pointed to an obviously unoccupied swing beside her.
She said no.
I jumped in the plastic saddle, held the chains so tight.

We didn't really talk.
We just swung there.
From time to time, we smiled at each other.
And, I'm not really sure whatever happened to her.
But, what I do know...
All these years later I'm still that little boy at recess.
I'm still scared to death of pretty girls.

−Cole.

Queen.

She is a *queen* and I want my face
to be her throne.

—Cole.

Fascinating.

I'm insecure the person writing the words isn't as
fascinating as the words themselves,
but that's why they make gin and grainy
filters and old denim in thrift shops and
black ink to tattoo my
off-white skin...

and if all else fails I can always kiss your neck and nibble on your ears
while we down two or three bottles of this rosé with a name I can't
pronounce. That'll make me fascinating, at least
for a night.

—Cole.

Gods and men.

I've come to know that there
are gods and there are men
and the only difference
between the two are the
women that raise them.

–Cole.

I tell him.

Honey, to tell you the truth, God and I's relationship is fairly complicated and I'm still trying to figure it all out. He says I don't call enough. I tell him the phone works both ways. And, then right when I mouth off to him, I'll find myself making a full-time living writing words at the age of twenty-three (now going on twenty-five) and I'll look up at him and say "touche". The two of us disagree a lot, most especially when it comes to that leather bound book in every drawer of every hotel nightstand in the country. I'll tell him I'm not sure if that leather bound book is truly him and he doesn't say anything. And then I'll tell him I wish he would have hired Stephen King or Ernest Hemingway or John Steinbeck or Virginia Woolf to write that leather bound book because I think there could be a little more prose and literary flair in there and he doesn't say anything to this either. And, finally, I tell him that it keeps me up at night thinking that my sweet grandmama never made it into heaven, according to that leather bound book in every hotel nightstand in the country and he keeps mum to this too. It's all very complicated and quite disagreeable. Yet, I do find myself returning to him despite our disagreements. I spoke to him the other night, actually. I said he did a fucking good job crafting your pretty soul and the next morning I woke up with a fever and a nasty cold. Part of me thinks it was his way of telling me not to curse at him even when it's complimentary. But I'm just thankful we agreed on something.

–Cole

Privileged.

A short story follows.

–Cole.

One—School Lunch.

I can't speak intelligently about white privilege. I'm not white. I can, however, tell you a thing or two about privilege. I grew up attending a high school where half the kids were white, half the kids were black and most of the kids were poor. I was an exception. At times, my high school reminded me more of a jungle than a place of education. My freshman and sophomore year there were a dozen police officers that patrolled the hallways at any given time, in case a fight broke out. And, they often did. I recall once biting into a slice of pizza and nearly choking as I heard a cracking sound rip through the cafeteria. I spun around and watched in horror as one kid grabbed another kid by the neck and proceeded to slam his face against the lunchroom table over and over again until it was a bloody mess. I think he would have killed him had it not been for a burly cop that tackled the pummeler, laying him out and then cuffing him. Since 50% of the school was on free or reduced lunch (some of the kids were so poor they'd wear the same clothes until they were riddled with sweat stains and matted down with dirt), I can't imagine the victim had the money to pay a doctor to piece his face back together again. When my school made the jump to school uniforms with the hope to end the vicious fighting, it wasn't the poor kids that complained, it was the rich ones because we had enough clothes to wear a different outfit for each day of the week. That's privilege.

–Cole.

Two—Swimming Pool.

I grew up playing basketball. I eventually went on to play at a small Division II school in Louisville, Kentucky for a year. I was good. Not great. But, I was good. A big reason I was good was because of a black kid by the name of Ty. He lived a few blocks away from me and we'd meet at an outdoor court during the summers and he'd kick my ass. My parents could afford to give me basketball lessons. Ty's couldn't. Yet, he proceeded to make a mess of me on that asphalt court under the hot summer sun day in and day out. A lot of people wonder why black kids are better than white kids at basketball. The racists joke it's because black people have an extra tendon in their calve that makes them jump higher. That's horse shit. Black kids are better than white kids at basketball because many of them grow up in rougher environments without a mom or a dad and sometimes without knowing where their next meal is going to come from. When you grow up like that, you become tougher, meaner and more aggressive in athletics. It has nothing to do with genetics. It's has everything to do with conditioning. White kids play sports for fun. Black kids play sports like they're going to war. There's a reason great basketball players like Michael Jordan have sons that don't end up being 1% the players they ever were. It's hard to become a killer on the court if you're learning to play the game in a big air-conditioned gym in a mansion. The world's greatest artists, athletes, entrepreneurs and creatives became great out of necessity, as a way out. With greatness comes riches and with riches comes rich kids and most of the time rich kids end up being underwhelming at best. I'd like to think I'll be an exception here (but that could just be my ego talking) because at the end of Ty and I's one on one games, I went back to a big house and jumped in my swimming pool. Ty didn't. That's privilege.

—*Cole.*

Three—Sweet Dreams.

My summer one on one games with Ty eventually made me good enough and tough enough to start varsity at my high school. During my two years on the varsity squad, I had a teammate named D. He was good. Very good. And, I would often tell him. I had played basketball with some great players. Ernie Duncan, Kendal Brown, Rontray and Dontray Chavis... (if Southern Indiana does anything right it breeds pretty girls, and boys that can play basketball). But, of the hoopers I had played with, D. was talented enough to be one of the best. After D. and I played our last basketball game together, I didn't see him for nearly four years. One day he and I ended up playing in the same pick-up game at a gym on the west side of town. We smiled when we saw each other, gave each other a big hug and played catch-up. His face lit up as he told me about his baby boy. He had just had him. He told me how he was going to be better for that child. He told me he was his whole world. I was proud of him. Four months later, at the young age of 22, D. was shot in the head because he was at the wrong place at the wrong time. I'm still alive because I grew up on a different side of town where you could sleep soundly at night without the fear of someone fucking you up. That's privilege.

—Cole.

Four—Rich Kids.

And I say all this not to hurt you. Though, I must admit, it hurt like hell to write. I say this to share with you the reality of the world we live in. I can't speak intelligently about white privilege. I'm not white. I can, however, tell you about privilege. Many of the people we see on Instagram like to pretend their lives are hard. Rich kids from Ivy league schools like to talk about how they had to "sleep on their mom's couch" while they built up their enterprise. Pretty white girls with fat asses and enough money to fill their faces with plastic like to bitch to their hundreds of thousands of followers about how "hard it can be having a following". Wealthy athletes and rap artists who haven't had to worry about money for three decades like to preach to America's influential youth about how important it is to live wild and free and to "not give a fuck". All of that is privilege. I know it's privilege because I grew up privileged.

And the truth is this—some of the people in this world, for no good reason at all, were born into extremely poor families in extremely dangerous neighborhoods where a hot meal is a luxury. And, as much as I want to look those people in the eyes and tell them it's going to get better, it's not always going to. So, if you're privileged, all that I ask is this. One, don't take it for granted and certainly don't waste it. Two, when you can, always, help someone who is less privileged. Three, remind underprivileged kids in your community that they don't have to become a professional athlete or a rap artist or Instagram influencer to make it big, remind them they can become writers, scientists, teachers, hair-stylists, designers, doctors and lawyers. You don't have to go out and start a non-profit, you don't have to go on marches, you don't have to change the world, you just have to change one person in it. Just once in your lifetime, look for some small way you can help someone who is less fortunate than you are. Because, to be completely candid, if you're reading this right now you're privileged too.

—Cole.

154.

Pajamas.

I've got a face you like to kiss on
and tattoos you like to touch
and words you like to read
but I'm really just a broken
little boy under all of this.

A broken little boy that wants to bury
himself in that waterfall you call a head of hair.

—Cole.

I can tell you what falling in love is like.

The loveliest aspect about falling in love is creating a new language. There's French and there's English and there's Portuguese and there's the Russian the pretty blue-eyed girls would speak to me in Belarus. But then there is the language each of us creates with our person. It takes time. It takes trust. It takes knowing a person deeply, intimately, for a long while. It takes falling in love.

At first, as the two of you develop your language, you won't even realize it. This is the fucking magic of it all. It's not unlike the native tongue you develop as a child, you don't remember learning it, one day you just wake up speaking it.

One night you find yourself at a dinner party, making eye contact with her and she bursts out laughing over something neither of you said just mutually understood. And, those around you who don't speak your tongue are looking at the two of you bewildered, like what the fuck is going on?

You begin to explain to them that it's nothing, just an inside joke of sorts, but you're lost for words because your brain is making your eyes dilate three-fold to absorb every millisecond of her gorgeous being; her face lighting up, her head going back exposing her soft neck and that laugh you want to hear echo through your head for the rest of your life.

This is when you'll know that the two of you have created your own language. After this, everything will change and you'll see this change immediately. The two of you will begin speaking without speaking. You'll hug her after a long day at work and her energy will light up your chest like hellfire and you'll know not to ask questions, but to just pour her a glass of wine.

You'll look up to find her looking at you on Thanksgiving like you're a snack and the two of you will leave the house, jump in the car and find a place far away from family to fuck. Suddenly, you'll start understanding her silences and acting accordingly. You'll know the silence that feels like the quiet before a storm is when she's about to cry. You'll know the silence that feels like Christmas morning is when she wants to stay silent longer and exist in that moment forever with you. You'll know the silence that feels like a lioness on the hunt is when you have to get her out of the room before she erupts on the mother fucker talking politics.

You'll know all of this without so much as a word and this is what falling in love is like. It's creating a new language with the most beautiful person in the world.

–Cole.

Cold hands.

She had a nose ring. I noticed it
when she said hello. She had long
black hair, too. It fell forever and was thick like
pounding rain. I ran my fingers through it because
we were both intoxicated and I knew
I would have always wondered what her
hair felt like if I hadn't. She liked it.
Or, at least I thought so. She smiled.
I wanted to make her smile more.
I shook her hand after letting go of her hair
and introduced myself. Her hands
were warmer and softer than mine and
I wanted them on every part of me.
I'm notorious for having cold hands.
My momma says it's because I have a warm heart.
She says that because it's what
`her momma used to say to her.

I thought about kissing her. In fact,
I almost did. I should have,
now that I think about it.

−Cole.

Taylor Spacey.

My homie, Taylor Mathis, looks weirdly similar
to Kevin Spacey and it's frustrating because
I feel like I'm the only one that sees it.

—Cole.

Kamikaze.

Love, I know you're looking at me like I'm a Kamikaze, piercing my way through the sky in a burning plane, craving death as much as I crave life. But, please know it's all more than that.

I'm not worried about a retirement fund or a pretty house with a picket fence or a 401k plan or "moderation" (what the fuck is moderation anyway). I'm not worried about what I'm supposed to be doing to prepare for three decades tomorrow because truth be told I don't think I'm going to make it until then.

I'm not here to create a legacy. I'm here to set the sky on fire like a shooting star, just for a moment. I'm here to light this world ablaze and then I want to be gone. Any extra time the reaper lets me stick around after that, well that's just cherries, love. That's just cherries on top.

I wanna fuck like a rockstar.
I wanna drink whiskey like I have demons to kill.
I wanna kiss pretty strangers.
I wanna run wild like a cowboy kid.
I wanna love my homies like brothers.

I wanna make so much money that I have to give it all away when I bite the dust. I wanna tattoo my off-white skin black so the mortician has some pretty pictures to look at when the music finally stops.

So, keep looking at me like that Love.

I am a Kamikaze.
Just know, it's more than that.

—Cole.

Cowboy kid.

I'm a cowboy kid, but I race on planes instead of horses.
I'm an American Kamikaze, I'm living with a death wish.
I'm a writer, chasing Hemingway knowing I won't catch him.
I'm a brother, to my brothers.
I'm a brother, to the beautiful souls that aren't.
I'm a dreamer, especially when it comes to that girl in the mountains.
I'm an addict, I'm addicted to pretty souls and pretty conversations.
I'm a sinner, though I'll be damned before I apologize for it.
I'm a runner, I'm running like I'm running out of time.
I'm a feminist, not politically I'm just obsessed.
I'm a demi-god, my mother is a goddess.

—Cole.

Probably.

When you feel something nasty
well up inside of you and you're on the brink of
exploding, step outside for a few minutes. It can
be hot or cold or neither. Freezing your ass off,
sweating your ass off or simply breathing in something
other than the situation making you see red has
a way of sorting things out. Ultimately, it helps
the rational side of your brain pose the question—
if I slapped this fucker with a phonebook,
would I regret it in the morning?

Probably.

—Cole.

Drown.

Falling for her feels like treading
water in steel toe boots.

I'm kicking my feet, fighting like
hell to keep my head above water,
but the harder I fight and kick and
tread, the faster I fall below her
surface.

I feel like I'm drowning in a sea of
her. *I want to drown in a sea of her.*

—Cole.

Ghost Story.

My great grandfather was a Japanese Shinto priest. Shinto is a religion that believes bad things are caused by evil spirits. So, most of a Shinto priest's job is spent keeping evil spirits away through rituals, healing and various practices. Most people don't believe in ghosts. But, I do. I do because they've bothered me and my brothers from time to time.

My grandmother used to say it's in our blood. I don't know. Anyway, about seven years back I was having some nasty run-ins with the supernatural and my momma got scared and bought me a sterling silver cross from Mexico with Jesus's face engraved in it. She then had it blessed by a priest.

Since lacing it around my neck, I don't get harassed anymore. I still deal with demons though. The ones I think up in my own head. The cross doesn't help with that. Nor does the cross prevent me from forgetting about church on Sundays nor does it prevent me from smoking cigarettes outside blaring bars, nor does it prevent me from drinking too much at those blaring bars, nor does it prevent me from going down on pretty girls.

And, I find it terribly ironic, because one day I'm going to die with it around my neck. My momma got it for me, after all, I can't take it off. And, when I die, I'm going to knock on those pearly white gates and the god the Christians tell me about will say the cross won't cut it.

Then I'll go down to hell and the devil the Christians tell me about will applaud me for my track record, but will say he doesn't allow crosses down there. And, I'll tell him to either let me in with it on or I'm fucking walking because my momma got it for me and it's not coming off.

He'll say no deal. And, I'll tell him to go to hell.

And, then, I won't be accepted anywhere, just the gray space in between heaven and hell. I'll be one of those ghosts my great grandfather used to shoo away. I'll be one of those ghosts my momma bought the cross to protect her baby boy from.

And, I'll be alright, as long as there is a pen and paper and a few books within arms reach.

—*Cole.*

Celestial.

Sometimes it feels like she and I are sailing through the milky way galaxy on entirely different spacecrafts, blazing through the black abyss at 17,500 miles per hour and with careful planning, copious amounts of fuel, blind faith and perhaps divine intervention from some celestial being… we'll end up on the same moon for an afternoon and if we're lucky for a weekend.

We'll just exist there, alone, just the two of us for a good while, watching the stars and the worlds and the comets go by, forgetting about our ambitions, and explorations, and dreams.

And, it'll be beautiful. It'll be the most beautiful moment in the universe.

And, then, one of us will decide it's time to go.

—Cole.

Space.

You are —

(keeping me up at night)

Like vintage Vogue magazine covers,

falling like snow from my bedroom ceiling.

Like black and white motion pictures,

projecting like dreams on the backs of my eyelids.

−Cole.

Hungry.

When I was a kid, I'd eat like it was going to be the last meal I'd ever have. For a long time, I wondered if I had an eating disorder. My grandmother shrugged it off as me being a growing boy (god bless her). It turned out we were both wrong. As I've gotten older, my hunger remains but food is now replaced with money, exercise, drinking, writing and from time to time when I'm not in an anxious spiral, sex.

While I wouldn't say I have an addictive personality, I would say my life is a constant ongoing battle of all or nothing. I can't just write, I have to write thousands of words a day. I can't just make money, I have to make as much money as I possibly can. I can't just have a drink, I have to drink until I am fucked up. I can't just go for a walk or a light run, I have to kill myself on the pavement.

My life is this wavering balance of extremes and to control myself, I avoid dancing on the line of moderation because I fail at moderation. Most days I will fast from the moment I wake up until 7 p.m. That's ridiculous but it keeps me skinny. During the week I won't touch a drink, because come Friday night I know I'll be losing my mind at some club. As for writing, I'm always writing, I'm never not writing. It is actually an addiction.

And, at times, I wish I were better at moderation. But, to be honest, it's just not the way I'm wired. I came into this world hungry and I'm going to die hungry and my hunger is going to make me wildly successful and ultimately lead to my demise and I'm okay with that. I don't want to be full.

—*Cole.*

X-mas.

Her
laugh
was
warm,
it
felt
like
Christmas.

–Cole.

Inspiration is a bitch.

Inspiration is a pretty bitch. She will show up when you least expect her to with a couple bottles of red wine and a pack of cigarettes. She will blow you away with her taste in music, poetically running her matte black fingernails along the spines of your vinyl. She'll throw on a record and fuck you good and keep you up all night long with delicious conversation.

But, there is a double-edge sword to her pretty and this is why you can't make a career out of her. She's unreliable. She won't pick up the phone when you call. She won't send you love letters. Half the time, you won't know if you'll ever see her again.

And, so, to creatives looking to make money in this game. I give this piece of advice… when inspiration shows up late at night on your doorstep run wild with her. But, don't for a moment, rely on her. If you rely on her you'll go broke.

Consistency, well that's a different story entirely. She'll love you harder than you've ever been loved before. But, you have to stay committed to her. You have to show up when you say you're going to show up. You have to call when you say you're going to call. You have to love her. You have to be loyal to her. Consistency makes a creative.

–Cole.

To my daughter.

1. Leave the world better than you found it.
2. Don't fuck around with a writer.
3. Don't listen to the words men say, listen to their actions.
4. It's completely normal if you like women, in fact, I'd encourage it.
5. Don't say 'I love you' unless you mean it.
6. *I love you.*
7. God exists, look for him outside of religious texts.
8. When you can, choose to love even when it's
   the hardest thing to choose.
9. Study: Sophia Amoruso, Rupi Kaur, Virginia Woolf & Coco Chanel.
10. Wear your confidence like Coco wore Chanel.
11. Find happiness in a room by yourself before
    you attempt to find happiness in a room with someone else.
12. You're a woman, you're playing with one arm tied
    behind your back, paint your lips and fuck shit up.
13. Before you get intimate with someone, imagine what it'd be like to
    have a kid with them (if you cringe don't get intimate).
14. Don't marry someone conservative, their discipline might be enticing
    initially but you'll find yourself loathing the closed-mindedness.
15. Ask your grandfather about your great-grandmother.

—Cole.

Locomotive.

It's 4 a.m.
I wake.
I'm sweating.
Again.
Just like the night before and the night before that.
A week prior I ask the doctor why while she is cupping my balls.
She runs some tests. Says I am healthy. She says it is my anxiety.
I eventually fall back asleep.
I wake.
It's 7 a.m.
I have five minutes of quiet before my mind starts racing.
It builds momentum slowly, like a locomotive.
But once it gets going it doesn't stop.
By 7:30 a.m., 6,000 tons of thoughts are screaming
through my skull like roaring metal.
I sit down. I begin to write.
If I write long enough and well enough, the thoughts become bearable.
When they become bearable I can live with them.
When I can live with them I can dance with them.
At 9:30 a.m. my therapist calls me back.
For an hour we work to make sense of these thoughts.
He has a big whiteboard.
He points to it.
He teaches me how my brain works differently than other's.
He says that's why I feel like I'm mad. ***I am mad.***
At 6 p.m. I'm having coffee with a pretty face.
I think to myself that it might be time to lay off the stimulants.
She comments on how calm I am. It's ironic.
If I am thankful for anything, it's that she can't see the war inside my head.

—Cole.

172.

Down the well.

I'm sitting at The Well in Nashville, Tennessee.
I'm at the long table by the big window with the view of Lipscomb.
A gentleman in a wheelchair rolls by.
He's young.
Not much older than me.
He's wearing a white polo.
It squeezes tightly around bulging tree-trunk-like arms.
That's what happens when your arms become your legs.
He stops his wheelchair.
Leans down.
Picks up a tattered piece of fabric in the grass.
He adds it to a pile of trash laying in a heap on his lap.
The trash is boisterous against his clean thoughtfully-ironed khakis.
I keep watching.
He keeps rolling.
Onto the next piece of trash littering this world he goes.
I start writing.
I start writing about how this gent can't use his legs.
But, is leaving the world better than he found it.

—Cole.

Arson.

She and I danced in the grey space between
fucking and lovemaking.

I'm not certain what you call it — *but it was*
something lovely — and we did this lovely
something with reckless abandonment like we
had nothing to lose as the room went up in
flames around us and we watched as our lives
spiraled into an inferno of our own creation.

We were arsonists with one shared interest, the
other person.

I'm not sure if you've ever missed someone as
you've fucked them, but that was this.

Every part of me was missing her as I was
grabbing for her neck and sifting my fingers
through her hair and running my lips along the
soft space between her legs.

We were both violent and gentle.

We grabbed and bit and licked and kissed.

We were tasting and feeling and breathing and remembering everything.
I think a part of us knew it'd be the last time we'd dance
in that burning room together.

–Cole.

Indigo.

If you've ever seen a denim maker's hands
they are forever stained this beautiful blue.
No matter how hard they wash and scrub
and rinse, the blue is ever there, ever present.
She was like that.
Like indigo.
There to stay in the lines of my palms
and the underbellies of my
fingernails.

−Cole.

Monet.

I'm fairly certain her back was the prettiest canvas I had ever seen. So pretty I can't imagine Van Gogh or Picasso or Monet or Rembrandt would have even bothered unpacking their brushes and palettes. They would have laid eyes on it, admired it for a good while and then they would have left. They would have walked right out the door through which they had come, shaking their heads whilst applauding a deity they had not known previously existed. Yes, that's how I'd describe it. I'm fairly certain her back would have made a famous atheist painter go to church on Sunday.

–Cole.

Breathe.

Don't apologize.

I wanted to drown in a sea of you.

—Cole.

On Belarus.

When you find yourself alone in a place where nobody shares your tongue you're overcome with mixed feelings of loneliness and adventure. Suddenly, the everyday easy, like getting a haircut, ordering a cup of coffee or asking a girl out to dinner feels like a solo ascent of Everest. However, despite this discomfort, I do think it's worth traveling alone from time to time, whether it be to gain a better understanding of oneself or a greater sense of confidence in one's ability to survive in the unfamiliar. This trip has been painfully beautiful. Lonely, yet lovely.

–Cole.

I'm not.

I'm not sad, really.

I just think a lot and sooner or later
when you do enough thinking
you stumble upon
your fair share of
sad thoughts.

—Cole.

My brother's keeper.

During my first week in Belarus, I met two gents from the U.K. whom I grew to very much adore. The three of us would stay up late in the hotel lobby and remark on how affordable wine and spirits where in Eastern Europe. We would then celebrate this affordability by purchasing a bottle of wine and then another and then another. The four nights we spent together were filled with conversations I will remember for the rest of my life. They left the country yesterday and today I'm overcome with melancholy. It feels a bit like finding out you have a pair of brothers across the world, having a four-day slumber party with them and then realizing you might never see them again.

–Cole

Hollywood romance.

Would you still love her if you couldn't post pictures of her?

Would that love still exist if you and she were the only two people in the entire world that got to experience what the two of you share?

I don't think so.

No, I don't think you would love her like you say you do.

I think the two of you are in love with the show, not the real people playing the actors in it.

−Cole.

Eve ate the apple.

The religious are quick to point
out the dangers of lust. But I would argue the creator
could have made it easier on all of us.

He didn't have to make her eyes
that lovely of a shade nor her lips so soft
and enticing. He didn't have to make
her hair so damn long and thick
and ever flowing.
The curve of her neck
could have been more subtle,
and her back less intoxicating.
Let's not get started on her hips,
that was a cruel joke
that set everyone in this world up for failure
before we even took our first steps.

Like Eve, I'm going to eat the apple and keep
eating it because it's sweet and
crisp and stunning.
And, if I'm ever
sent to hell because of it,
I'll be sure to send my
compliments to the chef.

–Cole.

182.

The things we leave behind.

It's going to be very interesting
as we get older and the people we
once loved so deeply have kids in
their arms that aren't ours.

—Cole.

Eough of the silliness.

From my experience, I can tell you that falling in love requires two things. One, you have to find your person. All of us have more than one person on Earth made for us regardless of what all the fucking fairy tales say. But, we should consider ourselves lucky when, by happenstance, we run into one of our people because it is rare. Or, at least I think so.

And, then, two, we have to be willing to love someone more than we love ourselves.

I would argue the latter is where the vast majority of people get in trouble.

–Cole.

Prenup.

A few nights back I was some kind of fucked up at a club in Chicago. I was drinking either a Moscow Mule or a gin & tonic. I can't recall what. I was dancing by myself in an area where no one was dancing. People were looking. One of the people looking was an attractive brunette who appeared to be in her early thirties. We made eye contact. She pointed a French-manicured finger at me, telling me to come hither. I did. I don't know why. I felt like I was in trouble. Like I was a little boy again and my momma caught me doing something I wasn't supposed to be doing. I stood a couple feet away from her still dancing. She asked me how old I was. I said twenty-five. She laughed, pretentiously. I asked why she laughed pretentiously. She said she only fucked around with older men further along in their careers. I laughed. I laughed because I never said anything about fucking around with her and because I had a plane to catch in the morning and because I was further along in my career than those further along in their careers. She asked me what I did. I said I ran a marketing business and wrote from time to time. She took one step closer. I took two steps back and turned around to go outside to smoke a clove that tasted like cherry kisses. I didn't ask her to join me. My momma didn't raise no fool.

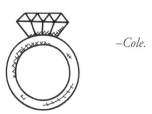

–*Cole.*

Almosts.

God, put me down early
with not a single wrinkle
on my face, just don't let
me grow old with a dusty
chest filled with
almosts.

–Cole.

Haunting.

You feel good sex long after you leave the bedroom.

It's a high that comes in waves.

It's an experience that becomes ingrained in your subconscious.

It's debilitating in the loveliest ways.

You'll find yourself driving, blaring Bon Iver when suddenly her fingernails run down the length of your back.

You'll be in the midst of a conversation with a friend and it'll be interrupted as her pouty whispering lips press against your ear.

You'll be falling asleep and snapshots of her will begin playing on the back of your eyelids like motion pictures.

Good sex is a ghost.

(It's a ghost you want to keep haunting you).

—Cole.

Henderson.

Powell, you're mere
moments away from beast mode.
I swear.

Just keep that head down
and that lense ripping.

–Cole.

China girl.

We were driving seventy. She was lost. But, confident despite her lostness. I was showing her my favorite songs on blaring speakers. But we never made it all the way through any of them. She would twist the volume to the right and to the left, indecisive about what she wanted more — to talk to me or to listen to the pretty songs I was showing her. That meant something to me, that meant the universe to me.

From time to time, the light from the sun would beam through the car windows, warming her face, transforming her eyes into a cascade of porcelain and dancing emeralds. It was bright that day and she eventually put her shades on. That hurt me. It felt wrong. Like she was covering up the prettiest art I had ever seen. I almost asked her to take them off (so I could look at them some more), but you can't tell a stranger you're in love with her eyes.

—Cole.

Cloud 9.

He took one look at her and then
he looked up, up, up... *he let Him*
know he'd be holding onto her for a
while.

—Cole.

On living.

One of these days I'm going to be dead and if my intuition is correct (which it generally is), it's going to be sooner rather than later. I'm going to go down in a plane crash or get smacked by a car or get an afternoon call from the doctor about something nasty growing in my chest. That's hard to read and it's hard to write. But, once you accept your time in this world is finite rather than infinite (meaning it doesn't last forever), you grant yourself permission to live with reckless abandonment. You start hugging your best friends and telling them how much you fucking love them and how goddamn gifted they are. You start buying plane tickets to fly five states over to take that girl you've been crushing on for years out to coffee. You start inspiring the beautiful people in this world to be everything that you know they can be. You start killing yourself to make good art. When you realize that you have mere moments to make the world a better place before you leave it, everything changes. Everything changes.

Please know,

everything changes.

–Cole.

But, I digress.

Cole Schafer

Most author bios are written in the third person which makes absolutely no fucking sense. If I saw someone talking about themselves in the third person at a dinner party (not that I attend many dinner parties), I'd think them to be an asshat.

Anyway, my name is Cole. I am a writer. I wrote this book. It's my first book. I plan to write a great deal more before I bite the dust. If you want to learn more about me, I'd take a peek at my Instagram (@cole_schafer) where I share pretty pictures (and words). Or, I would peruse my creative writing shop (www.honeycopy.com) where I work with brands like Google on writing words that don't completely suck ass to read.

Which, speaking of reading, thank you for reading. It made this little scribbler's heart burst with joy. I'd lick you but this is a book and you can't lick people through books. At least not right now. Perhaps in 2050. My God... will Fifty Shades of Grey be a wildly different book in 2050.

Anyway, cheers (and more cheers),

- Cole.

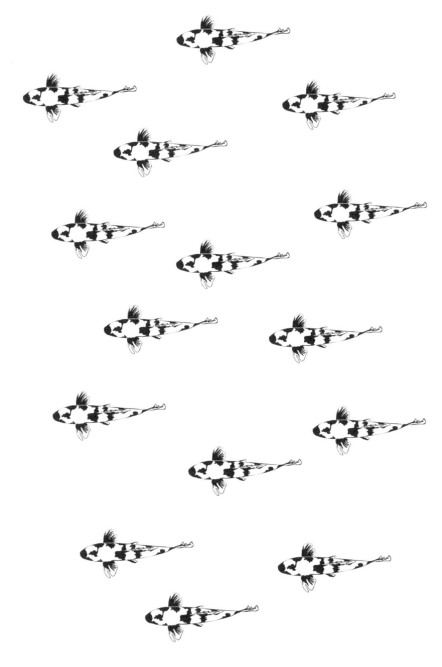

ISBN #: 978-0-9915282-6-4

Published and curated by:

Holon Publishing -
a collective of authors, artists, businesses, and creatives.

Holon Publishing
1311 Vine Street
Cincinnati, OH, 45202

www.Holon.co

Bulk ordering information:

Quantity sales. special discounts are available on quantity purchases by
corporations, associations, and others. For details on bulk orders, you may
contact the publisher at the website above, or by emailing
requests@holon.co

Printed in the United States of America